T0209108

Conversations *and* Encounters *with* GOD IN THE NIGHT

The Hidden Mystery Behind Dreams

TERRIE PHILLIPS

authorHOUSE

AuthorHouse™
1663 Liberty Drive
Bloomington, IN 47403
www.authorhouse.com
Phone: 1 (800) 839-8640

Published by AuthorHouse 12/02/2019

ISBN: 978-1-7283-3841-5 (sc)
ISBN: 978-1-7283-3839-2 (hc)
ISBN: 978-1-7283-3840-8 (e)

Library of Congress Control Number: 2019920251

Contents

Endorsements

In this brilliant book by my friend Terrie Phillips, you will discover how God works for our good while we sleep. Conversations and Encounters with God in the Night is easily the best book on dreams that I have read in years. With practical insight as well as supernatural disclosure, fresh understanding of God's sovereign night-work is opened. Woven into this book are stories which highlight the inner workings of God, bringing new keys to unlock the mysteries associated with dreams. Find out how God initiates real deliverance all by himself through a dream; discover how to prosper in your day-to-day life through answers received in the night; and learn about the Director, Playwright and Conductor of your dreams. You are holding a life-changing book!

Linda Anderson, Founder of His Way Ministries International

....

In this beautiful inspiring book, Conversations and Encounters with God in the Night, my dear lifetime friend, Terrie Phillips takes the reader into a deeper more meaningful understanding of how God is always intentional about communicating with us. Terrie's knowledge of God's design for dreams is not only biblically sound, but shows how God can use a dream to help guide us into discovering His design and purpose for us. In her book we come to realize a new excitement in looking for God's messages in our "maze" of day-to-day life. She also shows us how dreams offer a profound treasure hunt to inspire, encourage, and heal us as we continue on life's journey. Terrie not only has an eloquent way of expressing God's truths in this book, but she also has an amazing gift and ministry from God for the interpretation of dreams. This is a book that will awaken you to a deeper appreciation of your dreams.

Gayle Belanger, Counselor and founder of Live Free Healing Ministry

Dedication

First and foremost, I dedicate this book to my dad, my encourager and best example of God's love. You never wavered from your ability to love and extend grace to me (reflecting back over the years, I am sure I pushed the envelope many times over). While you might shy away from acknowledging your part, you taught me how to be a good listener and really consider the value of my words advocating "a gentle answer turns away wrath, but a harsh word stirs up anger." I love you Dad. There is not a day that goes by when I don't miss your voice, your words of encouragement and quiet strength of character.

Secondly, I dedicate this book to my son, Jason. From that first day I plunged into motherhood, you have been a constant source of joy. Could a mother be more proud of her son and his family – I think not! Your sense of humor mixed in with your tenacity to go after what you purpose to do in life always amazes me. The Marine Corp chose well when they made you an officer. Never wavering, you still exhibit all the traits of a good leader – bearing, courage, decisiveness, dependability, endurance, enthusiasm, initiative, judgement and the list goes on. I have no doubt the legacy you leave your son will inspire him to rise to even higher achievements. *"Ducit amor patriae"*[1]

---

[1] Phillips family coat of arms (a lion with a gold crown on a silver shield). Motto translated: "Love of country leads me.

Acknowledgements

A heartfelt and resounding shout of love goes out to my husband Steve for the countless days you prompted me to keep on writing. Many times I wanted to just push away the whole thought of authoring a book, but that part of your character that is persistent in nature kept encouraging me not to give up. I so adore that about you. Only you know how many unfinished stories take up residence on my computer and in your own succinct way you would smile and remind me that I needed to finish this one. You are the love of my life, my constant and best companion, my protector and steadfast supporter. I might also mention that you are the most knowledgeable when it comes down to retrieving valuable information I thought I had lost forever in cyber space. I thank God I met you at the little airport 45 years ago. Little did I know what an amazing adventure I would have sharing life with you.

A very special thank you also goes out Carole Heacock for helping me with every writer's nemesis, punctuation errors. Bless you, friend!

Introduction

God Encounters In The Night

Everyone embarks on a journey sometime in their life. Whether it is a simple road trip or a life-changing adventure with the potential to redefine your destiny it requires commitment, sense of purpose, a road map or two, and that innate ability to navigate new territory. Travelling long distances and putting up with challenges and obstacles along the way is par for the course, but knowing the final destination is within reach helps to inspire the confidence needed to stay on point. They say the joy is in the journey-that is often true. However, in my experience, some journeys may just take longer than others.

My personal route to understanding the mystery of dreams and the start of my journey began in the late 1960's while attending a well-known secular college in California. A college atmosphere introduces you to assorted and diversified types of information. You get to pick and choose. It did not take me long to realize there was a vital missing component – a deeper hidden meaning that I had yet to discover about the mystery behind dreams. The question that kept plaguing me was this, are dreams more than just subconscious random downloads of information competing with our conscious mind? I desperately wanted to know. I would not find the answer to that question or the missing component until several years later.

I was busy navigating college life complete with all of the challenges while also scoping out any information I could find on dreams. Over the years I had experienced many dreams that I could actually recall so here was my prime opportunity to explore the reasons for them. A large campus library full of books welcomed me in.

Long before the internet was even conceived, you had to work at finding proper resource material. The majority of what I found came from two well-known men of the 20th century – Sigmund Freud and Carl Jung. They were the most popular works of reference accessible at the time even though their opinions on dreams sharply differed.

Unbeknownst to me, a form of Western esotericism known as the New Age movement was also gaining momentum and merging into campus lifestyle. Any clinical or theoretical research I seemed to run across was slowly coalescing within a cocoon of psyche and metaphysical thought. Though widely popular, that school of thought felt too humanistic and I had a difficult time embracing any of it. Reflecting back on the philosophical notions of the time, I now believe the Lord was shielding me against a belief system that chose to remove the one true God out of the equation. It would take another 15 years before I understood what that truly meant for me.

Marriage and motherhood put everything on the back burner until a major life changing event took place – one that would change the course for me in words I cannot even begin to express. In 1981 I accepted Jesus Christ as my savior and began to read the Bible with increased interest. The books of Exodus and Daniel spoke of dreams and visions and it was amazing to me that the dreams of kings and men literally reshaped the course of biblical history. Something new and exciting began to stir deep within me and I found myself walking a new road of discovery-finding a path that would redefine the mystery of dreams, especially my dreams.

Like a beacon of light, I began to realize the Creator of the universe had been speaking to me through personal encounters in my dreams as far back as my early childhood. My long and arduous search for truth took on a much deeper meaning. I needed a solid foundation of biblical truth to move forward. Matthew 6:33 states clearly, *"but seek first His kingdom and his righteousness, and all these things will be given to you as well." (NIV)*

In the year 2004 I discovered Streams Ministries and the prophetic voice of John Paul Jackson. He was the leading authority on biblical dream interpretation and had developed a number of bible-based prophetic training courses of which dream interpretation was one. He was a pioneer in reintroducing back into the Christian community the importance of how God speaks to us through dreams. I had finally discovered a blueprint to aid me on my journey.

This was after all new territory for me and I must admit the training and practical experience period was often difficult. Some of those old concepts from my college days would sometimes try to overtake my thought process but I had developed a tenacious mindset and would not give in to discouragement. Even to this day I find myself referring to the Bible verse in Genesis 40:8-9 where Joseph was in prison and approached by two men who had dreams that needed to be understood. They said to him, *"We each have had a dream, and there is no interpreter of it."(NKJV) So Joseph said to them, "Do not interpretations belong to God? Tell them to me, please."* Three simple sentences helped me to push through and discover the missing keys to understanding dreams.

Joseph's statement to the two men that interpretations belong to God was a bold testimony of his faith in God. Joseph acted upon his faith and interpreted dreams trusting that God would give him all that was needed for understanding their complexities. He was willing to take a risk knowing that he also had received dreams when he was younger and acted upon them as revelations from God.

I began to understand that while experience is often the best teacher, a foundation of faith and hearing the voice of God is tantamount to success when interpreting your dreams and the dreams of others. I personally ascribe a lot of value to hearing and heeding God's voice when I encounter Him in a dream-those whispers from our Creator speaking to us as His captive audience.

My real life experience is by no means exclusive. There is still more to learn and maturity will always remain part of the process. Critical to my foundation building is this important truth-wisdom and revelations come from the Holy Spirit and I know He has a plan and a purpose in dreaming. A wise poet once wrote that a man's reach must exceed his grasp or what is Heaven for. It would seem to me that I have exceeded my grasp of heavenly mysteries many times over. Yet, I cling to the promises of God and keep moving forward knowing there are always new things waiting to be discovered.

That is the summation of how my journey began. With the technological breakthroughs available in our culture today, I am given an opportunity to finally put into writing my heart on the subject. All of the material contained within the pages of this book comes with my own personal touch. I am fully aware of the abundance of information readily available for those who are interested enough to explore the subject of dreams and their meanings. My focus and the mandate the Lord gave me for composing the material contained within the pages of this book is simple. God does desire to encounter you with conversations in the night. You just have to be willing to listen!

Chapter One

The Hidden Mystery Behind Dreams

"To sleep perchance to dream"[2] might be the most celebrated soliloquy from Shakespeare's famous play Hamlet. It would appear that even Shakespeare understood how important a peaceful night's rest is. I think that is why I love this particular line in his play. If you are a dreamer like me, you do look forward to turning off the light, snuggling down in your bed and peacefully drifting off to sleep. As a side benefit, there is always a chance you will have at least one or more dreams in the course of a night's sleep.

It is my belief that when we fully begin to grasp the meaning of our dreams a new connection is forged with the Creator of the universe. Acknowledging that God may be speaking to you through a dream brings encouragement to your spirit and quite often is like a prophetic statement just waiting to be embraced by you, the dreamer. The exploration of a dream takes on a whole

---

[2] "To sleep perchance to dream", Google search on famous Shakespeare quotes, http./ Literarydevices.net

new meaning. Ponder this verse in Isaiah 30:21 first and then read on: *"Whether you turn to the right or to the left, your ears will hear a voice behind you saying 'this is the way; walk in it,'" (NIV)*

What is a "maze" and how does it relate to dreams?

Twilight – that transition time between night and day and the few hours just before sunrise (astronomical dawn) when the sky slowly starts to get a bit brighter. As the sun gets closer to the horizon, the light still travels a far distance but it slowly becomes bright enough to wake up you and the world. For me, this is my best time for deep sleep and, of course, dreams.

Waking up prematurely will often find me struggling to piece together a dream I really need to remember. Getting up out of bed literally throws my dream to the four winds unless I can quietly remain there; taking time to ponder and pray for recall. People who wake up to an alarm clock or young parents with one ear tuned to the pitter patter of little feet understand this all too well.

I do not relish being left standing just outside that door to recall (metaphorically speaking). I can always sense something important, perhaps even life changing, is missing. I want to get back into the dream and at least have the opportunity to decode its significance, or not. This is quite often the mystery of dreams. You may never locate the entrance back in and even if you did would it look the same?

This type of speculation only benefits the person interested enough to take the time. I am merely using this as a useful example and visual on how a dream, its symbols, and metaphors creatively work together to weave a labyrinth of details and intrigue that can connect us to both our past and our present. There is always one way in and one way out. The adventure within is what poses the most mystery.

My dream (as an example)

I was standing in front of a maze, just a simple landscape and nothing more. I felt hesitant to enter because I knew I might get lost and never find my way out again. I questioned why I was even standing at the entrance to this maze and then quickly perceived that I could choose to walk away or take the risk to venture in. That was the context of my dream. There was no other interaction or people involved, but in its simplicity I learned something profound.

Up until that time, my only understanding of a maze reached back as far as what I have seen in movies. Those complex garden paths completely hedged in with tall shrubbery where the maze appears dark and foreboding and difficult to navigate through. At other times, a maze was portrayed like a garden scene with everyone confidently strolling through an interactive puzzle knowing there was sunlight at the end-perhaps even a prize. Good or bad, a maze conjures up many unusual scenarios.

I pondered that dream for days until the realization of its meaning became clear. The question most often presented to me by a dreamer is this, *"Why is my dream so perplexing, confusing and hard to figure out?"* While I could not always give a satisfactory answer to that question, my mind would keep wandering back to the picture of a maze. I could provide the analogy of a maze and its brief description as a means of comparison to the seemingly absurdness of a dream and the dreamer would instantaneously get both the picture as well as the answer to their question.

The definition of a maze as it appears in Webster's Dictionary is brief and helpful: *"An intricate, usually confusing network of passages....something confusingly elaborate or complicated....a state of bewilderment....stupefy, daze, bewilder, perplex."* [3] And yes, very similar in describing a seemingly illogical dream.

Granted there are deeper levels of understanding and objectivity in dreams that the mere representation of a maze may not even cover. In reality though, it is the strangeness of many a dream that often parallels a maze. Those are the ones we recall first hoping a quick explanation is plausible. More often it is not. There is no quick exit strategy-on to another day! Some dreams, like solving a puzzle or a riddle just require more introspection and waiting on the Holy Spirit for the answer.

When you read the Book of Daniel in the Old Testament you gain a better appreciation for how puzzling dreams can be and what may be required to navigate through the enigma of such dreams. I cannot reiterate enough how necessary it is to rely on the direction of the Holy Spirit. In Daniel 2:27 we receive very wise counsel from a man who lived through the challenges of his day. *"Daniel replied, no wise man, enchanter, magician or diviner can explain to the king the mystery he has asked about, but there is a God in heaven who reveals mysteries." (NIV)*

---

[3] Definition of a "Maze", Webster's the American Heritage Dictionary, Page 809

As the final epilogue to this chapter I would like to point out that when we are given a puzzle, a riddle or even a complex math problem, we set our minds to work. We become resolute in using time-tested problem solving methods that will provide both a solution and the final exit strategy. The process for interpreting dreams is really no different. There is a word from the French language, *nom de guerre*[4] that rather suits me. Before you rush to your dictionary, let me explain the meaning and why I chose to use it. A *nom de guerre* simply means a name chosen under which a person fights, paints, writes, etc., a pseudonym.

When I immerse myself in the complexities of a dream, I see myself assuming the role of a decipherer of puzzles and riddles. I engage myself willingly knowing that I partner with the **power of the Holy Spirit** and whatever I may encounter along the way, He will give me the inspiration necessary to decipher the dream. I literally assume all the roles of a *nom de guerre*: I fight for the understanding (because the logical brain will want to insert formal arguments that are often totally off base), I paint a picture for the dreamer that helps them grasp the meaning, and lastly I compose it all together on paper so that they have a written record of the dream. The mystery (and God) is always in the details.

---

[4] Definition of "Non de Guerre", Webster's the American Heritage Dictionary, Page 891

Chapter Two

"I Just Need The Facts Ma'am!"

Many people find it easy to stand on what we refer to as blind faith. Certainly, it means different things to different people, so I do not want to present that as a negative or disparaging comment. I have just found that many prefer more facts that can firmly lend credence to their beliefs.

Without a clear designation of factual information, they may be more inclined to close the book on further reflection. As a better demonstration, let me take you for a stroll back in time. I promise it will help give you a very clear visual of the role "facts" play when understanding how to interpret a dream.

Many of us are old enough to recall the detective series "Dragnet"[5] from the early days of television, circa 1950-1960's. Entertainment via television had not yet reached its' zenith, but it served a useful purpose in drawing families together in the evenings.

---

[5] Dragnet TV series "Just the facts ma'am", Google search, http./ Snopes fact checks

I remember sitting around our television on a Friday night watching the star of the series, Detective Joe Friday approach a witness and firmly state, *"I just need the facts Ma'am."* He always gave the impression that a witness would not be believable unless the pure facts were presented to him in no uncertain terms. Simple use of conjecture was out of the question for the detective.

How we process information (in relationship to dreams)

Recalling Detective Joe Friday's weekly comment about just needing the straight facts made me think long and hard about how people perceive information. Internal processors are more prone to mull over the facts of a dream and then methodically sort through them as a means to a solution. External processors pose questions immediately upon waking up from a dream. Through the process of expression they are much quicker to let go of anything they might consider superfluous rhetoric.

I am an internal processor, though at times I wish I took a more up front external approach. When I first began this pursuit I was very systematic carefully cataloguing information for future reference and then neatly tucking all of it away in a nice 3-ring binder. While appearing very thorough, this still gave me much angst. I felt I was experiencing a type of information overload that contributed to my internal dialogue screaming back at me *"I just need simple basic facts!"* I was becoming my own worst enemy by analyzing every little nuance and then frantically sorting through my reference notes. I was driving myself just a little bit crazy. There had to be an easier way and where was Detective Joe Friday when I needed him?

External processors, bless their hearts, find it easier to get down to the basic facts of grasping the purpose of a dream. They do not typically get frustrated with information overload because they process right away and out loud with other people. Therefore, they unload information immediately (good or bad) sorting through the facts by verbal exchange. Trivial information is rapidly excluded. I guess I could say something here like "good for them," but I would then have cause to repent.

Don't concern yourself with believing you need to process externally in order to interpret dreams better. Thinking that way will only cut short your flow of dreams. Surprise, both kinds of thinkers dream regardless so the good news is we do not need to over-generalize how we achieve the end results because in due time we can learn to pull from both sides of our brain. It just takes practice.

We begin to do this by understanding our strengths and weaknesses in certain areas and then adjust accordingly. The Holy Spirit will help us reign in and sort through the facts (symbols, metaphors, etc.) as needed. Grasping the concepts of how we process information is just one of the tools that will aid you in interpreting dreams. And by the way, the Holy Spirit is who I pull from now when sorting through a dream. He always has a way of cutting through the red tape by supplying the facts as I need them.

An important point to remember is this: One fact identified will not make you a dream interpreter! To aid you in the process of sorting through your own dreams, or the dreams of other, it is time to lay out some very important basic points as well as some of the most common questions asked regarding dreams.

I keep hearing about REM sleep – What is it and how does it affect my dreams?

I believe God created us to dream and those hours spent in good sleep mode are necessary for our body's health. Scientific research shows that dreaming occurs during the fourth stage of sleep, commonly referred to as "REM." This is characterized by rapid eye movement, increased respiration rate, and increased brain activity. The body though remains inactive to the point that you become actively paralyzed during REM sleep. Further sleep research reveals that we spend approximately 20 percent of our total sleep in this stage. Obviously God had a plan when he designed us to dream because we repeat the REM stages of sleep every 90-110 minutes during the course of a night.

In simple scientific terms, it goes something like this. At night our body cycles through different sleep stages. We usually move from light sleep to deep sleep, back to light sleep, then into REM where dreaming occurs. (Note: sleep cycles can vary naturally). During a REM cycle our bodies, at a cellular level, are at the peak of protein synthesis. This keeps many processes in the body working at optimum levels.

Light sleep and deep sleep cycles also serve a purpose. While you may or may not recall your dreams your body still does the work of dispersing information into a dream-like state as part of the body's process of repair. Deep sleep cycles have been shown to help strengthen your immune system while light sleep cycles take up more than half of the night. Lighter sleep cycles are important for the processing of memories and emotions and the regulation of your metabolism.

We now know that our brains process memories and emotions and our metabolism regulates itself throughout the night. I find it extremely interesting that during REM stages where most dreams occur, our brains are most active. This is part of the marvelous and complex biological system God designed to function while we sleep.

Does everyone dream because I am not sure I do?

Yes, everyone does dream. Typically, about 100 minutes per night. It is not something obscure and only experienced by a few select people. No! It has been scientifically proven that everyone dreams during the course of a night's sleep. Even though you may have difficulty recalling your dreams, you still do.

There might be one slight exception; mothers and fathers with newborn babies. Many of us can recall all too well those sleepless nights of waking up to a crying baby. We stumble into the nursery, change wet baby diapers by rote and with our eyes often closed, feed our little angels and then stumble back into bed hoping to catch a few more hours of needed rest.

How many times have I seen new parents with dark circles under their eyes wondering if they will make it through another night of baby bliss? Even I can still recall sleepless nights with a newborn hoping I might catch just a few more minutes of desperately needed sleep. When you love your children you take it all in stride but those REM sleep cycles are needed to restore and strengthen you for yet another day.

Why are my dreams so bizarre?

New research on the science behind dreaming has brought some interesting biological facts to the table. In their study researchers have found that those dreams that are most bizarre, vivid and emotionally intense are linked to parts of the amygdala and hippocampus.

The processing of emotional reactions with regard to memory is the amygdala's responsibility. The hippocampus serves important memory functions also by consolidating information from short term to long term memory. Why is this important and relevant to dreams? Because a reduction in REM sleep (that vital place where dreams occur) influences our ability to understand real life complex emotions which lends itself to the importance of how we react socially with our fellow man.

Dreams help you process emotions. Even though the experience within the dream may not seem real in its context, the emotions you experience are. Dreams displaying a lot of negative emotions can increase over time. This creates a reservoir of worry and anxious thoughts with nowhere to go and no place for expression, except thru a dream. Over time, the increased absence of consistent REM sleep shows a direct correlation to the development of mental disorders.

Your personal dreams may appear bizarre for a reason. The methods you choose to construct and retrieve memories (good or bad) while awake are the same mechanisms we utilize when dreaming. Evaluating the rest is best left up to you and the Holy Spirit.

Chapter Three

Where To Start

Developing a firm foundation

In one lifetime how many times do you think the word "foundation" has come up in conversation? It is a unique word and form of expression that has been used for centuries. Even today it carries weight (no pun intended) in our culture because it defines both past and future concepts of building structures, friendships, marriage, entrepreneurship, and biblical truths – just to name a few.

Furthermore, a foundation is used to provide us with a starting point, a sense of common ground, and a basis for mutual understanding. It is also fundamental whenever we begin to lay the groundwork for presenting our acquired knowledge on a subject (whether preliminary or advanced in study) to interested parties. For anything to hold up to scrutiny we always need facts and workable data coming together, flowing congruently, and with a strong platform to support that flow of information.

Begin to build from the ground up your biblical foundation of truth for interpreting dreams and you will be pleasantly surprised at the results.

It is an exciting world that we live in today with unlimited sources of knowledge readily available at our fingertips. Whether through the vast scope of the internet or a myriad of books, there are huge amounts of amazing scientific facts on how and why we dream. Unfortunately, there is one caveat. The rapid increase of the psychic world network has robbed many of understanding the biblical dimension of dreams. Many have had their hearts turned away from believing that the Lord still chooses to speak to us via a number of ways – including a dream (or a vision). This is all the more reason for you to have a firm foundation to stand on when people approach you questioning the validity of your beliefs.

Is there a biblical understanding for dreams?

Yes there is. Ten of them are referenced in the Old Testament book of Genesis alone. More are mentioned in the following books:

In Numbers 12:6, God declares that He would speak through dreams and visions *"When a prophet of the Lord is among you, I reveal myself to him in visions. I speak to him in dreams."* (NIV)

In Hosea 12:10, God declared that He did speak through dreams and visions *"I spoke to the prophets, gave them many visions and told parables through them." (NIV)*

God declared that He will counsel us at night through dreams and visions in Psalms 16:7, *"I will praise the Lord who counsels me; even at night my heart instructs me."* (NIV)

Furthermore, God has declared that through dreams and visions He will call us to change so that we will not perish. *Job 33:14-18 reads: "For God does speak — now one way, now another, though man may not perceive it, in a dream, in a vision of the night when deep sleep falls on men as they slumber in their beds. He may speak in their ears and terrify them with warnings to turn man from wrongdoing and keep him from pride — to preserve his soul from the pit, his life from perishing by the sword."* (NIV)

I can biblically point out several more dreams that were life changing for the dreamer and the culture of the time. A perfect example is in Genesis 41:15. Pharaoh had a dream that no one could interpret until Joseph was given the understanding. With His God-given ability to interpret Pharaoh's dream, Joseph's life changed dramatically as he went from the confines of prison to the palace of Pharaoh in a position of authority as his right hand man. As a result of one man's dream and one man's promotion, the course of history would dramatically change for the people of Israel.

In Acts 2:14 after Pentecost, Peter stood up with the eleven and addressed the crowd. He told them that this is what was spoken by the prophet Joel. *"In the last days, God says I will pour out my Spirit on all people. Your sons and daughters will prophesy, your young men will see visions, your old men dream dreams. Even on my servants, both men and women, I will pour out my spirit in those days and they will prophesy..."* (NIV)

Throughout the Bible, God has given instructions and prophetic revelations to His people through dreams. Everything written in the Word of God is still relevant for today and a standard to live by; and I have yet to read where God has chosen to close the door on communicating through a dream or a vision.

A vision and a plan for moving forward

Every journey begins with a first step. You would not have read this far unless you were hoping to increase your knowledge base about dreams. This is where having a vision and a plan cohesively works together. A vision sets in motion goals for the future. One would not expect to be successful in building a high rise apartment complex with only rudimentary drafting skills.

Even creating a profitable business with just a good idea is not sufficient enough to capitalize on without some kind of organizational plan. You need a strategy on how you are going to achieve your vision. Strategy is what we refer to as the plan. There are always steps to acquiring a workable knowledge base that compliments and adds depth to your foundational principles. 2Timothy 2:15 says *"Do your best to present yourself to God as one approved, a workman who does not need to be ashamed and who correctly handles the word of truth."* (NIV)

It is necessary to have a strategy (a plan with tactical insight) to achieve your goals. Furthermore, if you want to see the end result of your vision come to fruition, take time to survey the landscape around you. With discernment begin seeking out those speakers and writers who have successfully pioneered and developed methods for understanding the complexities of dreams. Consider that part of your foundational building and you can look forward to a future of understanding the concepts and mystery of dreams with better clarity and assurance.

Utilize your tools of learning

I once read a book that talked about discovering the spiritual meaning behind everyday events. That was an eye opener for me! When I started out on this journey of discovery I found myself overly cautious and very circumspect in my thinking. My awareness of God's presence in every facet of my life, both day and night, was limited to a very narrow field of vision.

To increase my awareness I began to reread the parables of Jesus in the New Testament. By doing this I gained new insight into how Jesus used symbols, imagery, and metaphorical language in a story. Their use helped breathe life into what might have been viewed as just an abstract idea. Powerful messages were conveyed through the use of a parable. Certainly a dream conveys a message in much the same way.

Seizing every opportunity to look up and out at my surroundings brought with it a greater discernment. The power of observation is a great tool. You don't want to miss what God carefully provides as a means of direction and insight by ignoring important signposts along the way. Tools are critically important to how we work. They enable us to put together, facilitate a process, and aid in communication of the Lord's intent for the dreamer.

Prayer is a priority

The prophets who interpreted dreams in the Bible always prayed first and then waited on the Lord to intervene on their behalf. That is foremost and of utmost importance to me now. I do not cut short the pondering time needed for each dream because in the pondering the Lord gives fresh perspective. With new heavenly insight I see things I missed the first time around and then I am able to step back and give the glory to God only. He is always faithful to fill in the blanks and give meaning to each and every dream.

Patience is necessary

Waiting patiently for the Lord to aid you with the understanding is wisdom. Being presumptuous never works but patience to wait on the Holy Spirit always produces fruit. Do you recall the TV series Kung Fu? The priest would often tell his young initiate, "patience grasshopper."[6] The implication was simple. Very little can be learned in a single day-there is no reward gained for being in a hurry.

I have had great mentors over the years and through their own experience I have learned the importance of patience. It has been said with some cynicism that praying for patience is a no, no. In this case, I would highly recommend it.

---

[6] Kung Fu TV series, "Patience grasshopper", Google search, http./YouTube

Taking time to record your dreams is another form of patience. If you merely hope you will be able to recall your dream later, do not be surprised if important details slip away from your memory. With each waking second, the context of the dream fades away leaving you with only snippets of recall. Keeping a dream journal and pen on hand by your bed is your answer.

In addition, keeping a record of your dreams and their interpretations is a resourceful way of gathering helpful information for future dreams. The more you recall, the more sense they will make. You will find you are better able to distinguish symbols and metaphors and patterns that repeat across a wide spectrum of dreams.

Keep things in proper perspective

We can easily become too fascinated with dreams and their interpretations. When we do this, we may find ourselves pushing the envelope of reality inviting the possibility of spirits of divination. That distracts us from the Lord's real intention and purposes of dreams. While God may not give us every dream, I do firmly believe that He is present in every dream. I believe this because He tells us in Hebrews 13:5, *"Never will I leave you; never will I forsake you." (NIV)* If He is always present then that means He is there when we sleep as well as when we are awake. Otherwise, He would contradict his word by slipping off in the night to attend to someone else abandoning you to the wiles of the unknown. That is not the God I know.

In conclusion, everything we seek to do in life requires proper perspective and balance. Becoming too overly captivated with our dream life has the potential to pull us away from what is real, absolute and unchangeable. Jesus Christ is my center and I hold fast to what He teaches us in His word. It is from that center that everything else is given purpose. It is vital to my relationship with the Lord that I convey His heart and His truth.

How can I begin to hear God's voice?

It took me several years and the realization that dreams are a tremendously important vehicle for hearing the voice of God. We need discernment though to make sure we are actually hearing God speak. Communicating with God is Spirit to spirit – not the way we know communication in our physical realm but by thoughts and impressions He gives us.

Our heavenly Father constantly desires to speak to every one of His children. He is always willingly to provide us with information and the guidance we need to overcome any problem we may face. We just need to be willing to receive it. He never comes up short on ways to communicate with us. Turn on your receiver, press in and seek the Lord on an intimate level. That is where encounters with him happen!

Chapter Four

Filling In The Blanks

•••• 🌀 ••••

You might ask what the word mortar has to do with understanding the meaning of a dream. Bear with me a moment while I define just what mortar is used for. It is a workable paste used to bind building blocks (i.e., stones, bricks, or concrete masonry) and a binding agent that aids in the process of filling and sealing any irregular gaps between the units. The primary purpose is to hold everything together when it hardens. Traditionally, mortar has been used throughout history. If you intend on constructing a sturdy brick building or wall, you will definitely use mortar.

Now let me bring that idea home. I had recently watched a special on the History Channel showing amazing structures situated all across the globe that are still standing strong even after several thousands of years. These pillars of construction would not be standing as monuments of ingenuity without the use of mortar. Architects and builders of old understood its necessity.

That got me to thinking about the necessary elements that *"bind"* together all the symbols, metaphors, colors, emotions, and parodies within a dream. While you might utilize some conceptual ideas, you still need something more *"concrete"* in order to interpret a dream. This is what we refer to as **context** and a subject I briefly referred to in chapter one.

Context – a vital component

Context supplies the brick and mortar to our dream world. It establishes the setting in which the concepts of a dream exists. Think of it as the big picture that gives credence to the circumstances and facts you are witness to. You can spend forever and a day studying the meaning of a particular symbol in a dream, but until you look at the bigger picture and how all the pieces relate together, you will miss the appropriate meaning.

I discussed earlier the importance of building a good foundation. Context will supply the substance, the connection, and the relationship that helps solidify your foundational principles when interpreting a dream.

By definition, the term *"context"* is, *"the circumstances that form the setting for an event, statement, or idea, and in terms of which it can be fully understood and assessed."*[7] Without fully comprehending the meaning of context you may find yourself stuck in a "maze" of confusion with no way out and no semblance of order to the dream.

---

[7] Definition of "context", Google word search dictionary

The importance of mapping a dream

This will excite all the left brain thinkers. You get to draw or diagram the key elements from a dream. It serves as a quick way to record a dream as well as help release your creative thinking process.

When I first heard of mapping a dream I instantly cringed. At times I can be directionally challenged when my husband asks me which way – east, west, north or south? My physical reply will consist of me pointing to the left or to the right – sometimes up or down which does not work in relation to our physical position on the earth with regards to north or south.

However, with our technical advances today, I rarely get lost crediting it all to GPS on my phone and in my car. You can look to the mapping of a dream the same way you look at GPS. It enables you to lay out and systematically group together the main theme and then the surrounding details as they relate to each other. It enables you to create a starting point while filling in all the blanks.

There are different concepts on how to map out a dream; however, I tend to use more of a linear or analytical thinking process. With this method I will print a dream out and then read through it in its entirety taking time to yellow highlight important symbols. I then define them in the margins as they relate to the context moving onto metaphors, descriptive terms, emotional highlights, active responses in much the same way.

With the addition of a lot of notes in the margins, that method has always worked best for me. It is a form of mapping in its own right. It just resembles an extensive on-the-page editing process of the dream once I have completed the interpretation.

Mapping or diagramming a dream, if it works best for you, will resemble those diagrams on sentence grammar you learned about in your high school English class. Flash back to your teacher asking you to find the subject, verb, preposition, etc. You group elements according to movement, emotions or feelings by drawing a square or circular pattern around each element. You will also need to establish the main character or focus of the dream and draw that in the center of the map. Draw lines or arrows to connect each square or circle as they relate to each other in the dream and to show the flow of action. I have included an example dream and then mapped it out using what is referred to as the "cluster method."

Example dream (cluster method-mapping): "*I was walking down a long hallway in my home. I stopped to look out a large picture window. I could see many strangers passing by my house and I wanted to go outside and meet them and then invite them in. I hesitated and realized my only fear was that they might not receive what I had to tell them. I turned and walked toward the front door and boldly opened it ready to approach anyone who would be willing to listen.*" Your example for mapping a dream is as follows.

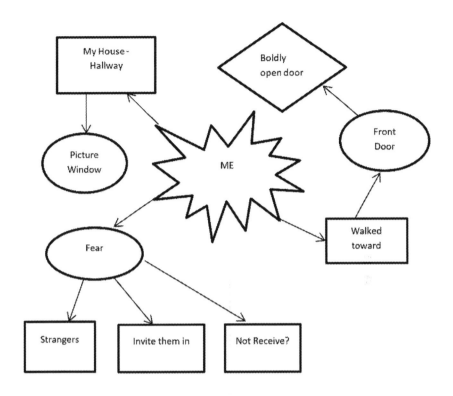

In perspective, the dreamer had a strong call on their life to evangelize and bring people to Christ. The hallway in the dream is symbolic for a time of transition for the dreamer. It was now time to take their calling out to the lost beyond the four walls of home. The Lord was giving the dreamer a vision for what would come if they set aside fear of rejection and were willing to be bold and approach those in need of Jesus Christ.

Whatever method you choose to aid you in mapping out a dream, your direction from the Holy Spirit must be the first source you draw from. Without His intervention, you are simply using your logic as a means to interpret. Revelation is the most important aspect of understanding a dream and revelation only comes from the Holy Spirit of God.

There are some important steps you take once you have completed the mapping of a dream. It is what I refer to as taking an inventory of your feelings. Your dreams are by no means flat line or devoid of the following characteristics: moods, emotions, physical sensations, reactions, sentiments and pleasures. They will easily resonate throughout a dream – you only need to identify them as they are presented.

Isolate the feelings (emotions)

Begin to evaluate the feelings of your dream by first isolating the emotions. You can refer to these emotions as the "cries of your heart". Ask yourself some basic questions about how you felt when you woke up. Some strong emotions to consider are: feeling sad, fearful, confused, lonely, angry, rejected, or threatened? Were there times you felt exposed, unprepared, frustrated, or disappointed with an outcome? On the lighter side and with a more positive affect, did you feel loved, excited, happy, content, curious, passionate, or hopeful?

It can be difficult, even painful to look at your emotions within the context of a dream, but they are an important messenger for the conditions of one's heart. Is there some aspect of your everyday life where you are feeling the same emotions? Taking time to ponder this will help you gain tremendous insight as to your dream's hidden meaning. If it is still not immediately obvious to you, ask the Holy Spirit to reveal it to you.

The symbolism behind actions

Actions are symbolic expressions in dreams. The term "actions speak louder than words" gives you a clue. How we act out in a dream supplies a boatload of information revealing our feelings, emotions, and perceptions. Here are some good examples: **Falling** can possibly indicate a feeling of losing ground in a situation. **Flying** can indicate a strong desire to rise above your current status. **Climbing** a hill with no end in sight can imply the struggle to get ahead. **Running** away from something is pretty self-explanatory. Fearfully watching your **teeth fall out** may indicate you are losing discernment. Looking for and then using a **toilet** suggests a need to cleanse yourself of some negative emotion(s).

The dream I diagrammed above for you gives a great picture of symbolism in action. The hallway was symbolic of a time of transition for the dreamer. Just think of what you do when you are walking down a hallway in your home. You are literally transitioning from one room to another. This same action is represented in the dream.

When you look out your windows in a dream you are looking for or at something outside the scope of your present reality. The larger world is calling out to you. Looking out a window is often symbolic for vision and the ability to gain a new perspective on life. Looking inside a window from the outside would signify something entirely different. You may be in need of some soul searching and introspection.

Is the dream about me or someone else?

When you dream about other people milling about, it is easy to think the dream is about them. Actually about 95 percent of the time the dream is still about you, the dreamer. Think of it like this: when you point your finger at something, you still have three fingers pointing back at you. The same thought applies to your dream. Your participation in the dream will help you evaluate the importance of your position.

As an example, let's say you keep having a dream where you are in a family group setting. The interaction of family members always seems to put you in the center of the conversation. While you may not even say a word, you are still a very important part of the context of the dream. Some family members are more vocal than others and it drives you crazy having to be in the middle of the discourse. You may think the dream is about your family member(s) inability to relate, but actually the dream is pointing out specific issues you are having difficulty with.

Even though the dreamer (you) are a quiet observer, emotions are spewing over throughout the dream. Feeling entitled to your opinions is a good indicator it may be time to readjust your position within the family dynamics. Your resistance or even participation when put in the middle of family conflicts may be affecting The Lord's ability to reach family members.

The eyes are our windows to the soul. If they only see anger and frustration in yours, they will not be able to see beyond those emotions. The Lord's grace and mercy will only appear clouded and obscure until they see it reflected through your eyes.

For the 5 percent of the time when the dream is actually about someone or something else, you will recognize it for what it is. You will be the observer doing just that – singularly observing from a vantage point away from the deeper meaning of the dream.

Even with this type of dream, you will still need to ask yourself if you are just choosing to isolate yourself from feelings of being overwhelmed by potential dangers. You may just be choosing to take a back seat, so to speak, and distancing yourself from any kind of interaction that you are ill prepared for. Pay very close attention to the context of the dream before assuming you are merely a spectator.

Flushing away the residue of the day

Some people like to refer to flushing dreams as "pizza" dreams. I am not a big pizza fan so I rather refer to flushing dreams as "goulash" dreams (a mixture of food that is not entirely appetizing). Those are the dreams of release that feel like a showering off of the encounters of your day. I always think of them as the kind of dreams that come cascading into my sleep in random snippets. I know they must mean something if I could only piece them together.

While it may appear fashionable in this modern age to dismiss the idea of good and evil, evil still seeks an advantageous foothold in good men and women. Flushing dreams are God's design to help us cleanse our mind, body, and spirit from the negative influences that want to attach to us through the course of the day. Daily we are bombarded by information and sensory overload and no way to avoid it.

We talked about culture as it relates to our dreams in a previous chapter. Well, just turn on the radio or TV and you get the picture of how much slime comes your way at the drop of the hat. Add accumulated demands on top of all that and you have a recipe for disaster (goulash)! The important question would be "*where does it all go?*"

Flushing dreams enable us to keep moving forward by removing the sluggish thoughts and emotions that might otherwise keep us stuck and not able to function at our best. For a better visual, take a moment to glance at your electronic devices. If you continuously ignore superfluous, even damaged, corrupted registry files on your desktop it may result in a severe crash of your IOS function. Oh, the infamous blue screen we all dread usually sends us running to the nearest Geek Squad.

I am thankful for the actions of flushing dreams because those day-to-day encounters would otherwise defile us if they were not washed off. We all are susceptible to picking up, unintentionally, those things that seep in to our memories. They would desire a permanent foothold if it were not for the actions of flushing dreams. In reality, we do not need to even piece together the meanings of such dreams. Appreciate them for what they are – God's grace and mercy disinfecting us from the residue of our day-to-day life experiences.

Chapter Five

More About Metaphors And Symbols

All dreams have foundational elements built within. They bring together the use of metaphors and symbols creating scenes and giving messages much like a parable. Most importantly, they reveal the culture of the day we live in.

Before I proceed any further let's take a moment to explore the actual meaning of the word "metaphor" and its sister companion word "symbol". A **metaphor** is *"a figure of speech applied to an object or action to which it is not literally applicable. A thing regarded as representative or symbolic of something else, especially abstract."*[8] Here are some good example phrases of metaphoric language: It's raining cats and dogs. Don't throw the baby out with the bath water. She has a heart of gold. I am literally jumping inside for joy.

By definition **symbols**, *"take the form of words, sounds, gestures, ideas or visual images and are used to convey other ideas and beliefs."*[9]

---

[8] Definition of "metaphor", Google word search dictionary
[9] Definition of "symbols", Google word search, Wikipedia

For example, the symbol for STOP is a red octagon. When we look at a map, a blue line often represents a river. Numerals are symbols for numbers and alphabetic letters may be symbols for sounds. Every culture will have its own identifying symbols as they relate to the spoken language.

When we attempt to understand the confusing and mysterious elements of our dreams, we discover that metaphors and symbols work simultaneously to create something that often resembles a **parable** *from the Greek word "parabole" meaning a comparison, an illustration, or an analogy.*[10] Depending on what message(s) your dream attempts to convey, you will experience any one or all of the above definitions.

The culture we live in

Considering how metaphors and symbols in a dream often present themselves in weird combinations, they are still taken from our everyday observations. In simple terms, we dream as we encounter life.

Dreams reveal the culture we live in. If you had lived in ancient biblical times you would likely have dreamt about chariots or donkeys; all those things symbolic to that period of history. Since we live in the 21st century everywhere we look there are automobiles, airplanes, cruise ships, military hardware, and last but not least technological devices galore. The average person's dreams will always utilize the information it is most comfortable and familiar with. In other words, what

---

[10] Definition of "parable", Google word search, Wikipedia

you see and hear on a daily basis will likely take up residence in your dream life.

Metaphors and symbols in operation

One of the best biblical examples of metaphors and symbols in operation is in Genesis 37:5-9, *"Joseph had a dream and when he told his brothers, they hated him all the more.....We were binding sheaves of grass out in the field when suddenly my sheaf rose and stood upright while your sheaves gathered around mine and bowed down to it." (NIV)*

The jealous brothers understood the meaning of the dream all too well. Symbolically the sheaves were a representation of the brother's future where they would one day bow down in total submission to the younger brother. Angry at their brother's forwardness, they took Joseph and sold him into slavery thinking to eliminate the cause. Assuming they would be rid of him for good they marched back to their father creating a lie to explain the rash disappearance of their father's favored son.

From historical accounts we know Joseph's dream would later come true. Even though a young Joseph was stripped of his position at home, many years later he would rise to a new position of importance in Egypt second only to Pharoah. In the end, his father and brothers would seek refuge from a season of drought and famine in Egypt; eventually bowing down to Joseph's position as Pharaoh's indispensable chief assistant.

This is a great example of a dream revealing the culture of the day along with the use of strong symbols and metaphors.

A parable for today

I have a good friend who shares her dreams on a pretty regular basis. That in itself is not unusual, but her dreams often border on the bizarre. So much so that I have to pull on all my dream resources and earnestly seek the Holy Spirit while down on my knees.

She approached me the other day with the gleam in her eye and I knew right away "Oh boy, here it comes!" Her non-traditional dreams often make me feel like I am suddenly thrust into an art gallery of surrealist painters. Salvador Dali's paintings are all around me and a college professor hovers over me waiting for an impromptu synopsis of the paintings.

This begs the question: Why are some dreams more peculiar in context than others? Even my own dreams seem relatively simple in comparison. So why are hers so different? I do know this; the meanings of dreams are a mystery and much like a game of hide and seek. It is God's invitation to pursue Him and gain a better understanding outside of our own basic logical reasoning.

It literally "stretches" my brain to gain insight into my friend's dreams. Suddenly I find myself simultaneously needing to utilize both my left brain and right brain functions. What a genius concept!

Thinking hard on this, I recalled that Jesus used parables as simple stories to illustrate a moral or religious lesson. Those parables used human characters in believable situations so that

His listeners would be able to relate the story to their current life.

I am in no way implying that my friend's dreams are solely being used to convey a moral lesson to me. However, they closely resemble the definition of a parable-juxtaposing (situating side by side) real life examples with very strong metaphorical and symbolic emphasis.

Rather unexpectedly, I now understood why many dreams are filled to overflowing with metaphors and symbols. It is first, a great way for God to get your attention. And second, it inspires you to dig deeper for understanding. God was consistently giving my friend those kinds of dreams knowing she would always be faithful to search out the matter.

In reality, she loves quilting blankets to give away as gifts so she is no stranger to putting unusual pieces of fabric together. Each piece of fabric has its own unique representation, but when she takes a scissor to the fabric and then systematically fits piece by piece small pieces of the original larger form, she is able to create beautiful landscapes of art.

Her dreams in a very imaginative way were often pieced together like a complex quilt; each one able to stand alone displaying the most unusual sequence of figurative expressions. Certainly in common with a fine work of art.

With my imagination in tow, sorting through the mystery of her dreams literally draws me in and I can see us sitting together on a Galilean hillside listening to Jesus speak in parables. In amazement we listen to Him pouring out love and wisdom through the metaphors and symbols in each story. Today I no longer look at her dreams as somewhat outlandish, but instead seek for the truths and wisdom of God represented through them.

What would classify as a modern parable for today might actually one day be your dream. Dreams are after all part of the Creator's design to illustrate or teach a truth, an important principle, or even a moral lesson. It is how He conveys a message directly or (sometimes) indirectly by the use of similes, symbols, and metaphors.

Chapter Six

All The Colors Of The Rainbow

We live and breathe in a world of color so why would our dreams be any less than colorful? It is a known fact that light changes speed as it moves from one medium to another. Even Isaac Newton's 1666 experiment of bending light through a prism demonstrated that all the colors already existed in the light continuously spreading out and traveling with different speeds through a prism. He further concluded that the prism did not create the colors but merely separated the already existing colors present in the "light".

In our dreams, colors often fan out like a prism with some more intense than others. Even muted colors serve a purpose within the context of a dream. They soften the tone of the dream serving to give greater emphasis to a particular person, place or thing you might easily ignore by the intensity of a specific color. We do need to pay attention to colors whether robust or muted as they appear within the dream. They will supply specific meanings like the road signs you encounter on a highway.

In Genesis 1: 1-2 we read, *"In the beginning God created the heavens and the earth. Now the earth was formless and empty, darkness was over the surface of the deep, and the Spirit of God was hovering over the water. And God said let there be light, and there was light. God saw that the light was good and he separated the light from the darkness." (NIV)* Interestingly enough, those words express a principal theme of the Bible. Whether physical light or spiritual light, a sovereign God declares that light will always have dominion over the darkness.

In our heart, we realize God desires to shed light on matters important to us. It only stands to reason that also includes our dreams. Through the darkness of night and through a dream, He spreads His light using colors to awaken us to our daily concerns. We relive situations and see them as a reality only visible and distinguishable with color. Without the necessary complexities of color, this would be a very dull world-one devoid of light.

Individual colors that vividly stand out in a dream are responsible for signaling you the dreamer. They can be objective tools showing you either positive or negative emotions. That is very important to remember when interpreting a color in a dream. Let me give you some examples.

Green: While we may see the color green denoting growth, prosperity, and life it is also a way to metaphorically show envy, jealousy, pride, or sickness. Think of the phrase "green with envy" or the "green-eyed monster" of pride that has reared its ugly head again.

Red: Symbolically red is the color of Love in our culture. It is also representative of passion. On the flip side it can show anger, embarrassment, even war and suffering.

Blue: The most utilized color to show revelation, heavenly insight, and communion with God. Famous painters across the centuries used blue and its many hues to give expression to the firmament. Depending how the color blue appears in a dream will tell you if it is instead a sign of depression, anxiety or sorrow.

Gold: By far, the most recognized color of kingship and also representative of the glory of God, purity, wealth of wisdom and illumination. Spiritually it can also show idolatry and a miserly intent.

Brown: Sometimes thought of as dull it is still a warm color representing steadfastness, dependability, compassion, and even humility (or) worldliness and dishonesty.

Silver: Silver is a precious metal like gold. Think of it in terms of redemption, justice, and valor. Also associated with prestige and wealth, it is negatively symbolic for legalism or betrayal.

Purple: Very symbolic for the robes of royalty and the dignity and wisdom that should go with it. Depending on the context, it may show a false authority, ambition or lack of moral discipline.

White: The color white is color at its most complete and pure state. It is the perfect symbol for the Holy Spirit. In addition it is a symbol for purity, awakening and innocence. With the absence of any other color it can show a religious spirit or sense of emptiness.

(Note: As an added reminder, you will of course, need to understand the "context" of the dream before making an assumption as to the meaning of a specific color.)

Dreams devoid of color

Just as color lends beauty to our surroundings, they also help paint a descriptive canvas in our dream world. The Italian painter named Elio Carlotti said it best: *"Beauty is the summation of the parts working together in such a way that nothing is needed, taken away or altered."*[11] But what if the canvas of your dreams is muted or even dark enough to give you a sense of foreboding?

Those kinds of dreams are always devoid of color and a place where we witness our emotions rise up to the surface struggling to find a sense of direction and peace. They give us a glimpse into the enemy's destructive agenda for our future; a warning to us to be more vigilant and sober. It is that internal struggle of darkness over light that battles to wash out any and all colors within the dream.

The truth is this. What you have trouble confronting in your waking hours continues to stir deep within our subconscious thoughts when you are sleeping. This would be the perfect time to recognize that the enemy's main intent is to kill, steal and destroy. If he can continuously keep you wandering aimlessly

---

[11] Elio Carlotti "Beauty is…." Quote, Google search, http./Urban Dictionary.com

in darkness, you may be deceived into missing God's perfect plan for you.

Believing the Lord is ever present and that He cares for you at all times offers peace. Receive comfort from this simple verse: Hebrews 13:5 says, "*for He, himself said, "I will never leave you nor forsake you."* (NKJV)

A very colorful dream

When I was a young girl I went through a period of being extremely introverted. There are four types of introverts: social, thinking, anxious and restrained. As an introvert, we can have varying degrees of the above traits. I had all of them.

Have you heard the phrase often alone, rarely lonely? That would also describe my childhood. My mother would often be vexed by my singular desire for time alone. She thought that I should be outside playing with friends, making new ones, and networking for the future. For me though, I was never too concerned for the future. I loved living in the moment and it largely required solitude.

When I referred to the Hebrews 13:5 in the paragraph above it stirred something deep inside of me. During my season of extreme introversion I had a very colorful dream.

I was about 14 years of age and in this dream I saw myself standing alongside a white split rail fence with a vast open field vibrant green in color directly on the other side. A tall white horse nudged closer to the fence where I was standing. Without hesitation I climbed the fence escaping the restrictions

43

it imposed, jumped on the horse and rode away feeling the wind in my hair and the strength of the horse galloping underneath me over the expanse of lush green rolling hills.

Total freedom without hindrance or restraint! How exhilarating! That dream was so simple in its design and the colors so intense that I almost felt I was awake while having it.

For years prior I had been experiencing many nightmares and dreams where I felt isolated and alone, chased by unknown assailants. I would then find myself escaping on a horse (usually brown in color) surrounded by a sea of muted semi-darkness.

I understand now that the enemy was trying to generate fear in me and heighten a level of anxiety that seemed to naturally surround me as part of my being introverted. Intimidation went hand in hand with my anxiety and I was always looking for a source of strength and courage that I could not yet identify with.

I loved God from a very early age but there was no one who could provide me with consolation for what my dreams meant or how I might take authority over them.

Surviving our teen years is always a cause for celebration. For me fear and intimidation would eventually take a back seat and then slowly wash away. I can't help but feel the dream of escaping on the white horse was part of the deliverance I needed. Over time, I finally grew comfortable in my own skin developing a new understanding that God had created me to be self-aware, not afraid.

As a perk, I gained an acute awareness of my surroundings and the ability to pick up little nuances like non-verbal body cues from others in a room. My friends now realize and accept that I just need more personal time and space than they do. It's no longer about a need to run away – but rather a chance to separate myself and recharge my batteries.

It is important to note that most people occasionally will experience the same dream over and over. When I learned to understand the message of my reoccurring dreams and finally do something about it, the dream changed and then finally ended. God's perspective then became my perspective.

Chapter Seven

Becoming More Aware

Having read this far, you are now more cognizant of a dream's importance. In addition to the basic foundational skills needed for interpretation, there are two significant categories of dreams you will want to add to your tool belt of knowledge.

Awareness of the categories will give you the ability to differentiate whether a dream is solely about you or something outside of your sphere of influence. I will refer to the two main categories of dreams as follows:

Internal (or intrinsic) dreams. They disclose specific information about you, the dreamer. You will recognize yourself as the main person involved.

External (or extrinsic) dreams. They are dreams that perceive outward information about people, situations or things rather than just immediate specifics about you. You are strictly observing.

Dreams highlight concerns and behavior patterns of life on a pretty consistent basis so it is helpful to understand whether a dream is designed to aid you in navigating life's journey (internal/intrinsic) or meant simply to draw you into a place of intercession (external/extrinsic).

Pay close attention to the sequence of emotions, characters, and symbols formulating within the context of your dream(s) and whether you are a participant or merely an observer and you will begin to better comprehend the difference between the two categories of dreams.

Dreams that disclose information about "yourself"

Self-disclosure is a process of communication by which one person reveals information about themselves to another. As mentioned above, we often refer to this type of dream as internal or intrinsic. Most dreams fall within this category.

Do you remember the simple rule of thumb? Point your finger at something and you still have three fingers pointing back at you. Dreams of self-disclosure communicate our internal identity; those heart issues that define your self-worth, purpose, and emotional state (even if there are other people emerging in and out of the dream). 95% of our dreams will deal with concerns of the heart. The mind, will, and emotions speak loud and clear in dreams of a self-disclosing nature.

Dreams that are motivated by "outside" events

Dreams of this nature are more commonly referred to as external or extrinsic dreams. This is simply the fly on the wall experience where the dreamer is just observing.

The Lord is not limited in the way He chooses to speak to His people. He will often use an external/extrinsic dream to reveal events (sometimes even catastrophic in nature) before they actually occur. Within the context of such dreams, you may be called to do something specific for the Kingdom of God.

Aside from the revelatory nature of a prophetic dream is, there is a common purpose. It is designed to draw us into intercession while making us privy to situations outside of our personal life experience. About 2-5% of your dreams will be external/extrinsic. The rest of the time dreams revolve within an internal/intrinsic realm.

I have provided you with an example of two types of dreams below-one from my own personal dream journal and one from the Bible.

My prophetic (external/extrinsic) dream

One month before the tragic events of 911 I had a dream, "*I was standing on a busy street and saw many policemen and firemen gathering close to a very tall office building several stories high. I distinctly remember the building because there were large glass doors for an entrance and very tall angular windows. There were firemen and policemen all around as I ran to go through the entrance. I was stopped by a fireman who thrust out his arm to prohibit me yelling "stop, you cannot go in there!" I could see the iconic and very familiar yellow police tape surrounding the entrance but at a distinct distance from the building. Something felt very wrong, yet I did not hesitate. I turned to the fireman and declared to him and all who could hear*

49

"but I have authority here!" as I continued to run toward the entrance to the office building." Then the dream ended.

On the morning of September 11, my husband called and told me to turn on the news because something very devastating to our country had just occurred. We all recall those vivid pictures of the two planes crashing into the Twin Towers, the people jumping from windows and the people running away from the towers before their collapse. We will never be able to forget the many policemen and firemen that risked their lives to save as many people as they could in the interim.

Three days later President Bush stood on the mound of rubble (ground zero) that was once the Twin Towers and had his bullhorn moment. "I can hear you" he declared. "The rest of the world hears you! And the people, who knocked down these buildings, will hear all of us soon!" The crowd of onlookers immediately responded by shouting "USA! USA!" In the background you see the steel structures and the blown-out window frames of the towers – the aftermath of the very structure I saw in my dream one month before the attack on America.

The reality of that nightmare moment has become an eternal memorial of what once was and is now. That dream still resonates in my mind and for a good year afterwards I would ask the question "why did I dream of a catastrophic event prior to it happening?" "Was I supposed to recognize something beforehand?" "Was there a deeper meaning for me in that dream yet to be uncovered?"

It took my Pastor's wife and a conversation about that dream to give me the clarity I needed. She said "God is sovereign." I had heard that spoken many times in my Christian walk but this day it took on a deeper meaning. Whatever happens, God is always in control, absolute, unrestricted, boundless and infinite. Nothing happens in the universe that is outside of His influence and authority. While the course of history may take an extreme turn, God still remains God and we may never fully understand why things happen the way they do.

I now know from research that I was not the only person around the globe to have a similar dream. As an individual, my dream was an epiphany moment. The word epiphany is derived from the ancient Greek word *"Epiphanea"*[12] meaning an appearance or manifestation. In literary terms it is that moment in a story where a character achieves realization, awareness, or a feeling of knowledge, after which events are seen through the prism of this new light in the story. For me that dream marked a future call to intercession and the awareness that no prayer goes unnoticed.

While our senses will often contradict what the spirit gives direction to, God's plans will never be thwarted. The very term *"Jehovah-shammah"* means "Jehovah is there." Even in the midst of chaos the peace of God can prevail and all things work together for an eventual outcome. You may recall that right after 911 thousands of people flocked to churches around the country.

---

[12] Definition of "Epiphanea", Google word search, Wikipedia

People needing to find peace and intercede for those who lost so much from the devastation.

As a result of that dream, my reality regarding prophetic dreams of catastrophes altered dramatically. Should the Lord choose to give me another prophetic dream similar to 911, praying for the people who might fall victim to such events would become a priority. I already knew I would be partnering with intercessors receiving similar revelatory dreams.

A warning dream from the Book of Daniel (internal/intrinsic)

Not every dream of a seemingly catastrophic nature may be revealing future events. Negative events in your dream may be what we refer to as a "warning dream." Those kinds of dreams are your opportunity to take proper action and change the course of events hopefully in your favor. God's intent is always to show the dreamer that they can change. We can have influence over a negative event thereby changing our circumstances to a positive outcome.

My favorite example of this is in the Book of Daniel. The young man Daniel lived in the courts of King Nebuchadnezzar in Babylon and he was gifted with the knowledge and understanding of both dreams and visions. In Daniel 4:1-36 the king has a very vivid dream of a tree. Toward the end of the dream (4:13-17) a very clear warning is given to the king, "*I looked and before me was a messenger, a holy one coming down from heaven…..Cut down the tree and trim off its branches; strip off its leaves and scatter its fruit…..let him be drenched with the dew of heaven and let him live with the animals among the plants of the earth….till seven times pass by for him." (NIV)*

After Daniel had systematically laid out the interpretation of the dream as the king had shared it, Daniel gave it as a warning to the king. It was time for the king to renounce his sins by doing what was right; to be kind to the oppressed in his kingdom and then the king's mental stability and prosperity would be regained. As the story goes, the dream was fulfilled exactly as Daniel had interpreted it.

In conclusion

Two categories of dreams were just revealed to you in this chapter; one prophetic and the other a warning. One was a revelation to the observer in the dream (extrinsic) and the other a call to change their direction in life (intrinsic). Rest assured that in the course of your lifetime you will have multiple intrinsic dreams and perhaps even a prophetic dream or two. Pay attention and take time to record them. The more you do, the more the Lord will reward your diligence.

Chapter Eight

Nightmares And Night Terrors

Resting vs tribulation in the night

The other night I had a very graphic kind of dream. One of those I would put into the category of a nightmare. Instantly I was awakened from peaceful sleep with my heart racing and a mournful cry escaping from my lips. No matter how old you are, some dreams contain just enough of a frightful edge; enough to make you fearful and feeling like a child again.

At the end of that dream, I heard the Lord gently say to me "Do not be fearful" and then I saw him put a very large flashlight in my hand. While the presence of the Lord was telling me to not be fearful, I sensed that He was also telling me to turn on my flashlight and point it directly into the darkness. Whatever internal battle was raging around me that night was instantly extinguished by the light and washed away by comforting words from the Father. Once again I was able to return to a peaceful, restful sleep.

As adults, we usually don't fret too much about an occasional nightmare and tend to disregard them once we get busy with daily routines of life. The most common thought is to just shake it off. For children, it is altogether a different matter. Instinctively they realize the need for sanctuary and the loving arms of a caring parent speaking reassuring words of peace over them.

It was that particular nightmare that made me ponder my own childhood night terror dreams. To this day I can still recall a vivid night terror dream at the age of seven. It was so terrifying that I immediately jumped out of bed and ran for the sanctuary of my parent's bedroom only to feel some unseen force holding me back. I was frightened out of my wits, unable to utter a single word, while fighting to reach their room. Someone or something was holding me back causing me to remain rooted to the floor of my bedroom.

What was the force holding me captive? I still do not know the answer to that question except that it took my father turning on the light in my bedroom and his reassuring deep voice to quiet my fears and make me feel safe again. Light dispelled the darkness that surrounded me!

It is important to note that God spreads light through the darkness and that the darkness has no power over the light. That is the very nature and character of our Creator. The book of Genesis 1:1-3 reveals to us this truth, *"In the beginning God created the heavens and the earth. Now the earth was formless and empty, darkness was over the surface of the deep and the Spirit of God was hovering over the waters. And God said 'let there be light' and there was light. God saw that the light was good, and he separated the light from the darkness."(NIV)*

Regarding nightmares (and night terrors for children) it is necessary to shine a light on the matter even if it means handing them a flashlight to keep next to their bed as a symbolic gesture. Wrestling and struggling can take hold in the darkness of night. In Daniel 2:22 we read, *"He gives wisdom to the wise and knowledge to the discerning. He reveals deep and hidden things; he knows what lies in darkness, and light dwells with him." (NIV)*

From the moment of your creation, God has seen potential in you and set a plan and a purpose in motion to fulfill it. This very potential can be thwarted by subconscious fears and painful life experiences. Those generational curses and deeply hidden things will often reveal themselves in a nightmare. However, God wants to call you out of your history and back into your destiny by pulling out any evil intentions so that you can be put back on the path He designed for you from the beginning of your inception.

In simpler terms, the sequence of a dream is much like the planting of seeds in a garden. We sow seeds down into the dirt where they lie hidden away from the light. With rich soil and proper care in due time it is the very light that causes those seeds to reach upward and begin to burst forth with fruit and flowers.

Much like a garden, we are all born with seeds of greatness, not mediocrity. We need to be relentless in going after what God has put in our hearts from the moment we were born. Our dreams need the revelation of God's light so that nothing remains hidden away that might destroy our potential for a fruitful future.

As an adult, we may have an occasional nightmare plague us. While we may not need to jump up and turn on the light to dispel the darkness of the dream, we do need to explore the powerful dimensions of the dream. Is there a warning we need to heed and what are you discerning about your dream that is throwing up red flags all around you?

There is also the added dimension of a reoccurring nightmare. Quite often it is the best way for the subconscious mind to send us a rather strong message. Our soul (the mind, will and emotions) may not want to hear it, but internal warning bells keep going off. Be honest with yourself. We can look at the reoccurrences as one way of inducing excitement so that our spirit will ponder the dream enough to make needed changes. They do not need to be feared if you see them as a way to provide helpful suggestions toward a better and more peaceful life.

God may also be developing your ability to take authority and set right events in your life that have the potential to spiral out of control. It may even simply be that God wants to give you strategies for the spiritual warfare that currently surrounds you. Any type of graphic imagery in a dream has a significant purpose-it encourages us to look at our fears and realize the power they may hold over us. Maybe even strategy to win the battle.

A few common nightmares and their explanations

Naked in a public place: Who hasn't had this particular nightmare at least once in a lifetime? It is the type of dream that we immediately wish we could forget, and also the type where we recall every embarrassing, sordid detail and sometimes in full color!

Nothing is worse than being totally visible when you would rather appear invisible. If you know the people in the dream, the nakedness compounds itself because you sense the foolishness of the situation as you attempt to grab some non-existent towel or piece of clothing.

The first clue to understanding the dream is "vulnerability." That word comes from the Latin word vulnus for "wound". It is the state of being open to injury, or appearing as if you are. In your waking life you may be lacking confidence and a fear of being exposed or weakened in some capacity.

There is always a risk to opening yourself up to possible criticism. Ask yourself this question: What are you trying to cover up to minimize the risk? This might be a good time to realize that transparency is not a weakness because when you have nothing to hide or conceal you do not need to fear vulnerability.

<u>Someone or something is chasing me:</u> A very common nightmare that tends to be very metaphorical in nature. You may see yourself pursued by either an animal, a person, or even what feels like dark forces. At the start of the dream you may even feel rooted to the ground desperate to secure a means of escape. Emotions run high and confusion is usually a strong part of the nightmare.

A nightmare of this nature can be a wakeup call for the dreamer. Do you want to take control of your life, but it seems impossible to do so? Are there issues related to self-esteem where you sense someone is putting too much restraint on your life? They may be exhibiting hostility toward you in subversive way. Instead of facing a situation directly, the dreamer is often choosing avoidance in the form of running away from potential confrontation.

If an animal is chasing you and it is wild in nature, then look at the type of animal and what dangers it can represent. There could be an emotional issue raging within the dreamer. Take time to observe the many facets of your dream. If you cannot figure them out with the help of the Holy Spirit then it could mean deeper issues that need guidance and/or counseling.

Help, I am drowning: This kind of nightmare is a good indication you are feeling deeply overwhelmed or drowning in some goal or expectation in life. Literally feeling like you are way "over your head." Coming to a more secure place where you can openly express the emotions behind the feeling of being overwhelmed will, of course, help you.

Another aspect of a drowning dream may be the need to rescue people from overwhelming circumstances you become privy to. I once had a dream of swimming in an unusually large lake. There were people scattered all around me and only my husband and myself were able-bodied swimmers in my dream. I longed to bring each and every one back to the shoreline, but I was unable to accomplish that large a rescue.

This dream taught me a good lesson. Regardless of my capabilities, not everything is under my control. Sometimes it is just about letting go and allowing God to intervene for you.

Fear of falling: Plummeting to your demise is never a good thing. At least in a dream you can rest assured that you will wake up before impact. This type of nightmare gives a pretty clear message depending on whether you are falling, slipping, jumping or being pushed by someone. Any way you look at it, a dream of falling will often reveal that you have lost control over some aspect of your daily life. My husband once told me parachuting out of an airplane cured him of this type of dream. It might have worked for him, but what if you do not relish the idea of jumping out of a perfectly good airplane?

In order to put the puzzle pieces together you must first determine what kind of falling you experienced. For example, say you were pushed and then fell. This could imply that you are being pushed to your limits by someone in your real life.

A dream of losing your balance and then falling into the unknown is a very common dream. It might indicate you are feeling very unstable and unsure; maybe even feeling like you are losing your grip on life. Falling into an unknown and uncertain future can be very disconcerting. Taking time to assess your emotional state when awake and how the people in your life directly influence you, both good and bad, will give you clues to dreams of falling.

There can be many reasons why you dream of falling, but how you land reveals a flip side. If you land on your feet, this shows you have the ability to overcome obstacles with a realistic approach. If you find yourself gliding safely to the ground, then you subconsciously realize there is a better way out of a difficult circumstance. You just need time to figure it out.

Bathroom dreams: Often seen as a kind of flushing dreams (how apropos) these are dreams of a very intimate nature. They usually involve three aspects: Toilet dreams, shower dreams, and bathrooms in a public place dreams. They suggest a need for a cleansing of messy situations in our life. Something has negatively impacted you and you have a sense of urgency to quickly eliminate it.

The inability to locate toilet paper or a clean, secluded bathroom might simply mean you want to cleanse yourself of having to put the needs of others before you. Circumstances are not allowing you to do that and you just need to find a space away to figure it all out. Privacy would be the key word here. Especially if in the dream you are unable to locate a bathroom with doors.

Dreaming of taking a shower in private or in a public place reveals a strong desire to be thoroughly cleansed from a problem. Ridding yourself of things that have negatively impacted your life is a good enough reason for this dream. Find a bar of soap and some shampoo, and you are on your way to a fresh start.

Whether they are about spiritual things or physical things, bathroom dreams exhibit a wide spectrum of much needed awareness on the part of the dreamer. Be sure to examine any negative as well as the positive implications in the dream.

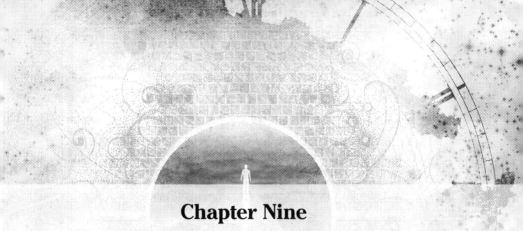

Chapter Nine

Dreams Of Healing

•••• 🌀 ••••

A dream of physical healing

For several weeks I had been experiencing pain in my left leg. Numerous trips to the chiropractor were short lived. I knew I was healthy enough to eliminate any other physical reason so I remained clueless to the source of the pain. On some nights the inflammation in my leg was so excruciating it would keep me awake just trying to find a comfortable enough resting position.

During the day I was beside myself desperate to find a remedy. Too much Google research makes you believe you are privy to any number of symptoms. I believe in prayer, so I prayed like crazy for healing feeling overcome and worn out by the whole thing. Oddly enough, on random less-painful days I would hear that still small voice whisper to me *"quit thinking so much about this – it is a distraction that wants to keep you in a place of fear."*

I realized that whisper was speaking truth to me. When I did not pay attention to the pain, it ceased to concern me but the moment I got back on the pain train, I felt it hit with force again. It felt like an internal battle I was apt to lose. Yet daily, I continued to hear the Holy Spirit urging me to let go of the fear and stop embracing it.

After a few months of dealing with the pain, I had a dream. In the dream *I saw myself standing on a hillside. The hillside offered no secure footing and as I began to slide down to the edge of a cliff with a deep ravine just below, I sat down on the ground and grabbed hold of a stake in the ground to keep from sliding further. I cautiously glanced over the edge seeing nothing but a very dark and formidable canyon below. As I glanced back up the hillside I saw and heard a man speak very calmly to me. "See the threat for what it is and stop being afraid of the danger it represents or it will pull you into the abyss. Grab hold of this stake, plant it firmly in the ground and use it to pull yourself up and out of this. I am waiting for you up here."* I did just that in my dream and then promptly woke up.

Several days later I was given the meaning of the dream. Metaphorically speaking I had been carelessly walking a hill of doubt and fear struggling to find a way out of the pain. Nothing was working and just when I would think I was pain free and successful in my endeavors, I would slip back down and have to deal with the pain again. My fears in the dream were represented by a canyon of painful emotions-very dark and formidable and symbolic of an unknown future of pain and discomfort.

In the days that followed every time I felt my mind wander back to thoughts of leg pain, I promptly saw myself grabbing hold of that stake in the ground, digging in and pulling myself up and off the cliff to stand before the man I saw in my dream. 1John 4:18 speaks to my spirit whenever I recall this dream. *"There is no fear in love; but perfect love casts out fear, because fear involves torment."* (NKJV) In case you are wondering, Jesus was the man standing on the top of the hill.

Needless to say, the leg pain has ceased to give me grief. Through that dream I am now more aware of the things that would divide and distract me from feeling strong, healthy and able to do the things I love to do. My focus on the things of God has returned with new fervor and all because of a dream.

I do realize that many suffer with pain of varying degrees and you may not truly understand how a simple dream could bring you said relief. What I really want you to grasp is the fact that God was speaking to me about my situation long before the dream. I was just ignoring what He was saying.

It is my firm belief that if He cannot get your attention when you are awake, He can certainly get your attention when you are asleep – and through a dream. If you are willing to pay attention, they are one of many vehicles of communication the Lord may use to send you a message.

A dream of emotional healing

I love Disneyland just as much today as I did when I first entered those magic gates at the age of seven. You can throw off the cares of life and for a few brief hours revel in the joy and fun of fantasy, heart dropping rides and great food. All of it is great with the possible exception of one ride. You will instantly recognize the ride in question because of its ability to leave a lasting imprint on your neural pathways.

This Disney ride commonly known as "It's a small world" plays the song "it's a small world after all" from beginning to end, over and over again! By the time you exit you will undoubtedly recall this signature song for hours, possibly days, and even years to follow. Walt Disney had a purpose and well-planned strategy when he allowed the implementation of this song into his theme park.

Why am I bringing this up, you ask? Because it makes me think of the kind of dreams that seem to hit repeat more than we care to have them.

We call those dreams "reoccurring dreams" and there is a definite reason why we have them. They re-occur because we did not hear and act on the message of the dream when it spoke to us the first time. They will continue to show up from time to time until we are able to work through whatever situation gave rise to the dream in the first place. Much like that Disneyland ride and the song attached to it, reoccurring dreams keep popping up when you least expect them to. Pay attention!

I had a reoccurring dream that went on for many years. I would find myself walking through streets in San Francisco with the simple aim just to get home. I would also feel frustrated in my dream because every time I turned a corner or crossed a street, I felt like my journey was taking much longer than it needed to. I would think should I find a car to take me where I needed to go, but I had no car keys available anyway.

There was such an urgency to get home, but I felt helpless to get there. I would periodically enter a department store to look around, but even this diversion did not ease the fear of getting lost on the streets of San Francisco late at night. Even the people wandering in and around me offered no support for my situation and when I approached them they would merely turn and walk away.

The crazy thing about this dream is that I grew up near the City by the Bay. I frequented those streets too many times to mention in both car, bus and on foot. I knew my way around. So why was my dream feeding me such negative information? Silly me, I never bothered to answer that question and flat out refused to dig any deeper into the meaning. Denial had reared its' ugly head and I chose to partner with it for many, many years.

One non-eventful day I was sharing my dream with a counselor friend of mine. She sat back for a moment pondering my dream and then she asked this question *"In reality, has this ever really happened to you in San Francisco?"* Of course it had and suddenly I flashed back to a time in my history when I was a young expectant woman of 20.

Please note: This piece of history reveals events from my first failed marriage. My husband of today (Steve) is a wonderful man and we have been married for 45 years now. He only asked that I clarify one thing – he is not the husband referred to in my reoccurring dream. My first marriage was ill-fated and while there were many hurtful situations I could easily recall, for some reason I chose to keep buried deep in my subconscious one very significant event.

Back to that moment of revelation with my friend and the recollection of a traumatic memory: I saw myself standing out in front of a department store on Market Street waiting for my husband (at the time) to pick me up. It was growing late and the store was getting ready to close. I was also 7 month pregnant and very tired on my feet. After putting in an eight hour workday, I just wanted to be home resting, not waiting on a lonely street corner in the dark of night.

He never showed up and I was forced to walk many, many blocks at night to a Greyhound bus station far from where the department store was. It would then take me countless more hours in a Greyhound bus before I eventually arrived at our apartment. I was scared, exhausted and also very angry at the whole incident. I chose to avoid confrontation that night and days after. I was never able to really forgive him or the situation surrounding it.

Flash forward to the present. I had pushed the memory of it all so far down into my psyche that it seemed inconsequential to my life at present. Except that I would periodically have those dreams of losing my way in the city, watching it grow darker around me. I always felt desperate and confused, not to mention at times angry at myself for not having a clearer picture of my surroundings.

My friend gently suggested that now was the perfect time to forgive and let go. I had to laugh but also ponder why it took me so long to figure that one out. I did just that in her presence and instantly felt the Lord lift off the memory of that night. My emotional healing was complete although I also had to repent to the Lord for being stubborn in ignoring the signposts the Lord had given me in that dream.

Even a dream interpreter may miss it. Significant to my healing was this realization. Feeling entitled to anger, painful regrets, and hurts can keep you a prisoner. Rehearsing and re-immersing myself in disappointments that are part of my history draws me back into that shell of denial. No one truly wishes to remain a victim. I am happy to report that since that day I have not had that reoccurring dream again.

In conclusion, challenges brought to the forefront of our waking moments often prefer to remain hidden. Our filters tell us "not now" and "I can't deal with that at present". If this is the case (and it often is) then a dream is just another avenue the Lord uses to release a suppression of memories and emotions needed for introspection, and yes, even possible healing.

God has no limitations on what and how He pursues us. I love what Psalms 23:6 says about how the Lord loves us, *"Your beauty and love chase after me every day of my life."* (NIV) I believe God designed us to receive those revelations of who He is. It is also His prerogative as to when and how that may occur, so why not through a dream.

In conclusion, dreaming is part of our DNA. All across this planet Earth everyone dreams so there must be something significant about it. Beyond our logical reasoning, it begs the question, why would our Creator equip us with such a tool? I believe it is about His pursuit of us and a very real and personal quest to be relational with humankind both in waking hours as well as sleeping hours.

Chapter Ten

Moments In History And Sparks Of Creativity

Aristotle once wrote *"All men by nature desire to know."*[13] Human history records this statement to be true but does not simply imply that the human mind seeks only to understand the scientific. While we have become explorers of both nature and the universe around us, we also yearn for deeper understanding of God, infinity and eternity, and the philosophical questions of how our mind, will and emotions influence our connections with one another.

This creative force within us – this quest for knowledge has given rise throughout history to artists, inventors, entrepreneurs, writers, and scientists alike. Many have solved problems and found their creative spark through their dreams. This is just a small sampling. You will find many more by doing your own search of dream inventions, creativity and scientific inspiration.

---

[13] Aristotle quote, "All men by nature desire to know", Google word search, http./ The internet Classic Archive

The sewing machine

Elias Howe was an American inventor of the sewing machine. Our grandparents and great grandparents took full advantage of Elias Howe's invention because up to that point it was thread and needle or a tailor who made clothing. Even my grandmother had the old style Singer treadle sewing machine tucked away in her basement.

In 1845 Elias had the idea of a machine with a needle which would go through a piece of cloth. This machine had the potential to shave off countless hours of intensive labor by hand but he just couldn't figure out how exactly it would work.

His first attempts proved futile but then one night he dreamt he was taken prisoner by a group of natives. They were dancing around him with spears and then he noticed that their spears all had holes near their tips. How interesting that a dream of this nature would bring about a piece of machinery able to shave off countless hours of labor and in addition, create an industry for clothiers around the globe.

When he was awake, he realized that the dream gave him the solution to his problem. He located a hole at the tip of the needle on his machine so that the thread could be caught after it went through cloth. His sewing machine then became operable. The sewing machine was created and the rest is history.

DNA, The double helix structures of deoxyribonucleic Acid

Scientist James Watson and his research partner Francis Click discovered the structure of DNA but it was in a dream that James Watson saw a spiral staircase. That dream helped launch a whole new perspective on what "deoxyribonucleic acid", the carrier of genetic information looked like. What a perfect visual to something not seen with the naked eye.

What vital elements of research would we be missing today if this discovery had remained hidden? God truly did have a plan. So much research has since been done on DNA helping to launch criminal investigations and further research on genetic information. That spiral staircase picture of DNA is well recognized today and all because of a simple dream.

The periodic table of elements

In 1869 Dimitri Mendeleev, a Russian chemist and inventor of the Periodic Table of Elements, had been spending months trying to find a logical way to organize all the known chemical elements. He had written the name of each element down on a card with their properties but he was still looking for a better system of representation. Thank goodness for persistent people with a logical mindset!

While at his desk, Dimitri fell asleep and a dream came to him with a more formal arrangement of the elements. The current system of reference cards everyone had been using were thrown away.

The Periodic Table of Elements, well known to us today, was centralized and unified into one simple chart. I can almost visualize mathematicians and scientists of the day standing up and tossing hundreds of reference cards up in the air while rejoicing over that discovery.

The ever famous E=MC2 equation

Albert Einstein is known by just about every one across the planet for his famous equation on the Theory of Relativity. But did you know that according to this famous scientist this concept came about by way of a dream? Einstein's theory asserts that time travel is possible when energy and mass are equivalent and transmutable (changed from one form, nature, or substance into another).

His dream went like this. He saw himself hurling down a mountainside. He gazed up at the starlit sky and that's when he noticed that as he sped faster and faster, approaching the speed of light, the appearance of the stars changed. While I am not sure I would have received the same exact revelation Einstein received, the scientific community is certainly glad he did.

This dream was unique to his scientific mind and offered Einstein insight into the nature of the universe. For me, this is a probably one of the finest examples of the incredible creativity and scientific revelations inspired through a dream.

A better golf swing from a dream

Pro golfer, Jack Nicklaus has shared with many how he perfected his gold swing through a dream. Back in the day, my own father who was an avid Jack Nicklaus fan and golfer would have loved to have had that kind of dream.

As the story goes, Nicklaus had been experiencing a slump in his game back in the 60's. A lament any golfer dreads but especially so if you golf for a living.

In 1964 he had a dream that he claims inspirationally helped to improve his then famous and tournament winning golf swing. In the dream he saw himself hitting the golf balls fairly in line with how he wanted them to go. Suddenly, he realized he was not holding his club the way he actually held it at a winning golf event. That would become a moment of revelation that only an expert golfer might recognize.

That dream might not have been so amazing except that Jack was perfectly in tune to what was needed for a tournament winning golf swing. He knew he had been having trouble collapsing his right arm and taking the club head away from the ball. However, in his sleep and in the dream he was doing it perfectly. The way it should be done to win at golf.

The next morning when he entered the course, he utilized his club the way his dream showed him and it worked famously. Golfers around the world were taking note of what had changed for Jack Nicklaus. He was able to shoot a 68 and then a 65. His slump was sufficiently over from that point on. The rest is history and written down in the golfing hall of fame. No doubt, my Dad even tried to copy that award winning swing.

The discovery of atoms

Niels Bohr is a Nobel Prize winner well known for his discovery of atoms. While we may not see them with our naked eye, we all take for granted the presence of atoms. It was through yet another dream that Bohr was inspired to perform a series of tests to confirm the vision he had received through a dream.

One night in a dream he saw the nucleus of the atom with electrons spinning around it like the planets do around the sun. In every classroom across America today we learn that atoms are the basic units of matter and the defining structures of elements. Thank goodness for a persistent scientist leaving a legacy for generations to come.

What to look for in the future

Now you might not have a vested interest in looking for a dream of invention. I myself have had dreams where a myriad of equations and numbers flashed by in a dream (mostly common numbers of 7, 1, 2 and 3). Yet, I am not a mathematician by any stretch of the imagination.

My dream in question took place in a long hallway with classrooms lined up on one side and several picture windows on the other side. Above each door were plaques with classroom numbers in no particular order – classroom #7, classroom #3, classroom #1, and classroom #2 clearly visible to me. I sensed there was no real urgency to find a particular classroom because I knew I would eventually enter all of them in the not too distant future. I was more inclined in the dream to look out the picture windows first.

Knowing this I suppose those particular dreams will not readily give evidence to future complex answers for mankind, at least none that I am currently aware of. For me, it was more a dream for vision.

Dreams can become a vehicle to your destiny. In that season I was stretching myself in every way possible to acquire a workable knowledge for dream interpretation and at times my learning curve experience resembled a six lane highway replete with multiple exits. I was becoming more acutely aware of the Holy Spirit's presence and needed a vision(s) that would tell me I was on a true course. All my classrooms had numbers symbolic of God's presence in the learning process. That became my reassurance that God was indeed guiding me along.

From that dream I have learned that you should never write off odd occurrences in your dreams as some strangely curious aberration. You could find yourself having more than one dream with similar quirky symbols and by simply putting them together, be pleasantly surprised at the outcome. God may use such an anomaly as a future blueprint for some extraordinary life adventure.

The anomaly of numbers in a dream

You will never escape the significance of numbers. Their importance literally rests in the hands of our Creator. Psalm 147:4 reads, *"He determines the number of the stars and calls them each by name."* (NIV) When you look up into the vastness of a dark clear night sky (away from all city lights) you instantly become overwhelmed by your own inability to count the number of stars visible to your naked eye. Even when you utilize a telescope, that same feeling grows exponentially.

With that in mind, I determined to specifically include the significance of numbers in this chapter alone. I tread lightly here because I do not subscribe to anything bordering on numerology, the paranormal or an association to astrology. We cannot, however, ignore the fact that the Bible is full of God's arithmetic and He uses numbers extensively as a way of speaking to us in His word.

The number "7" is but one of many examples used in both the Old and New Testament. It is the number of completion. The number "3" is symbolic for the Triune God, Father, Son and Holy Spirit. We see the number "40" with reference to a trial, time of testing or probation. Israel was in the wilderness for 40 years; Moses was in Midian for 40 years; and Jesus was tested in the desert for 40 days and nights. The number "50" signifies a time of jubilee when the Holy Spirit was poured out on the day of Pentecost – which was also 50 days after the resurrection of Jesus Christ. Numbers are a high level form of symbolism in the Bible. They have always been an important way God speaks to us.

If your dreams reveal numbers, then seek wisdom for their meaning from the Holy Spirit. Remember that while numbers do have significance, we need to avoid making them mean more than they are. Refrain from the use of numerology because that could open a door into the realm of divination.

Chapter Eleven

Legacy: Training Up A Generation Of Dreamers

•••• ☄ ••••

When we read or hear the word "*legacy*" we understandably think of our heritage, our birthright as passed down from generation to generation. Yet, the meaning behind the word "legacy" expands further beyond its definition.

As an example, the Founding Fathers and Framers of our great country proposed to set in writing a rich legacy for the nation we live in. Out of their desire for a unified country our Declaration of Independence and Constitution were birthed.

While the main motivation might have been for the prosperity of their immediate families, the legacy would extend far beyond their original vision. Several Founding Fathers were instrumental in establishing schools and societal institutions that still exist today. Their faith-their beliefs-their legacy have been the focus of historians for the last two plus centuries.

The point I am trying to make is this. Our Founding Fathers held freedom near and dear to their hearts. The core of that belief was the right to life, liberty and the pursuit of happiness. Even though that belief would ideologically be challenged many times in the years to come, at the center was man's faith in Jesus Christ.

They believed they heard from God. When we see it written "One Nation under God" on buildings around Washington DC, we are witness to that legacy left by the men who had courage to speak it as well as write it thereby establishing a strong foundation of truth for generations to come.

Hearing the voice of God through dreams is also a legacy worth sharing. It will always be about seeking the Giver (our Lord); never just about the dreams or visions. We ultimately seek to serve God – not the gift.

That is the legacy we want to pass on to succeeding generations because we too, hold near and dear to our hearts how the Lord speaks to those who will listen and what it means to interpret what He is saying.

An Old Testament biblical legacy

The well-known patriarchs in the Bible all had a legacy of dreams they passed on to succeeding generations. When Jacob, an Old Testament patriarch, left Beersheba and set out for Haran he had a dream where he saw a stairway reaching from the earth up into the heavens. He also saw the angels of God ascending and descending on the stairway. In that dream he saw and heard the Lord give him specific instructions relating to Jacob's future descendants.

He was given a future glimpse of the legacy he would be leaving for generations to come. *"I will give you and your descendants the land on which you are lying....all people on earth will be blessed through you and your offspring. I am with you and will watch over you wherever you go and I will bring you back to this land. I will not leave you until I have done what I have promised."* (Genesis 28:10-15) (NIV)

That dream prompted Jacob to set out on a journey that would change his life and set in motion dramatic outcomes directly influencing the formation of the Jewish nation. His youngest son, Joseph, would carry the legacy of dreams forward with a prophetic insight of future events concerning his brothers and father.

Again, that legacy would develop an open door for Joseph to eventually interpret the dreams for the Pharoah of Egypt. Nothing is ever by chance but all by God's design.

A New Testament biblical legacy

I could go on with more biblical information on the relevance of such a legacy by just projecting forward hundreds of years recognizing a different Joseph of the New Testament who had two very significant dreams. In the first one an angel of the Lord appeared (Matthew 1:20-24) and told him do not be afraid to take Mary home as his wife even though she had already conceived through the power of the Holy Spirit.

In a second dream (Matthew 2:13) and after the birth of Jesus, an angel of the Lord again appeared to Joseph telling him to take the child and his mother and escape to Egypt where they would be safe while Herod, thinking he would have to give up his throne should the child grow to adulthood, searched for the child to kill him.

Each dream helped shape the future for succeeding generations. What God had ordained from the beginning of time would not be thwarted by adversaries bent on destroying that legacy of saving grace brought to us through the death, burial and resurrection of Jesus Christ.

My path – my legacy

I have had many conversations with God through dreams and the marvel of encountering God in such a unique way still leaves me speechless. Worth noting was one very short but inspirational dream that propelled me forward into writing this book. In my dream, I saw myself sitting at my computer hearing the voice of the Lord whispering to me these words, "*it is not all clinical (*pertaining to dreams*); it is also personal* (from the heart)." That was another epiphany moment where I realized the Lord was urging me to write from my heart my own personal experiences regarding dreams.

For five continuous mornings thereafter I woke up with the names and contents for additional and very specific chapters. I had received a very personal invitation to communicate the heart of God about dreams and an avenue to share my legacy for dream interpretation. . Ecclesiastes, Chapter 3:1 reads: "*There is a time for everything and a season for every activity under heaven."* This was my time to begin.

Looking back, I am humbly reminded that a very creative God desires relationship with his creation. It is who we are and how He has made us that has enabled mankind to progress from dwelling in caves to exploring the infinity of space. That baton, our legacy as children of God, passes from one generation to another in one singular and powerful driving force – *"The eyes of the Lord are on the righteous and His ears are attentive to their cry."* (Psalm 34:15) (NIV)

The responsibility for carrying a legacy forward may rest solely in your hands. Whatever the case, you carry within your spirit an image of God's purpose and specific destiny for you. Ask yourself what does that look like – how do you fit in with the grand design? No other person is better designed for such a time as this than you.

It does not matter whether you are in a training phase or simply curious about how God communicates with you. Dreams present us with a multitude of possibilities. They can direct us toward what is beneficial for our life or help warn us and redirect us away from harmful situations. They can provide inspiration or even a pathway that may set you on that pilgrimage of a lifetime.

Mankind needs wisdom. If we are to make wise choices with all the uncertainty we face day to day, we need Holy Spirit revelation.

From the very beginning of time we have been given a legacy of dreams. It was God's design for his creation and a way to keep us on a path of spiritual health. Becoming that relational with our Creator brings us securely back into a place of intimacy that clearly defines God really does know and care about us.

If He designs a dream specifically for you and you realize it beyond a shadow of a doubt, then be courageous enough to understand its meaning. You just may be catching a glimpse of your own personal legacy.

Final Thoughts

From A Purely Personal Point Of View

I often marvel at how a dream in the night can mysteriously unfold a story line comparable to any popular movie and/or good fiction novel. Even the simplest of dreams can create a basic plot full of drama, unique individuals, colorful landscapes, humorous dialogue, embarrassing encounters, or moments of dreadful suspense.

The creative mind of God has no limitations and since we are created in His own image, why would dreams not flow with the same endless possibilities. Just gaze around you and then begin to ponder the vastness of the universe and you will be overwhelmed with the likelihood anything is possible with God.

As I bring to an end this book, I wanted to stretch your imagination just a little. You can either choose to fit yourself into the characters of "my dream story" or just take the seat of a casual observer. You get to pick. I will only ask one thing of you. Pay close attention to how the Director, Playwright and the Conductor work together with the placement of the characters on stage and behind the scenes.

My one disclaimer is this: It is from my perspective only because I am hoping it will spark a sense of curiosity on your part to want to delve deeper into the complexities of dreams. In a real sense, it is a dream written out in story form. I hope you enjoy it!

A dream and an allegory with a twist

My stage name is "Believer" and there have been too many sleepless nights just waiting in anticipation for this moment. I enter stage right where immediately I am aware that all the expansive scenery and necessary props needed to convey a complete picture are finally in their appropriate place; everything strategically placed for human interaction. My supporting cast of characters is ready with their personal lines memorized and fully ready to engage.

Even the stagehands are behind the scenes awaiting their turn to facilitate the shift of scenery and props when needed. Everything serves a purpose and nothing will be left unattended. The orchestra, under the expert guidance of the "Conductor," acknowledges that all rehearsals have been completed to the satisfaction of the "Director" and "Playwright." Music, much like worship, is an important element aiding the audience in feeling the highs and lows-the specific mood of the play at critical stages along the way.

I take my position on stage and I feel my heart as it momentarily skips a beat. This time I am the leading actress, not a supporting actor/actress, and not just an observer. Everything will rely on efficient interaction with my fellow co-actors.

As the leading actress I grasp how important this is to delivering the key message of the play as intended by the Playwright. It is vitally important that I convey the proper emotion(s). One slip or incongruent response will have a rippling affect.

Every spoken word and every calculated movement across the stage has an explicit purpose. The Director has personally conversed with me many times and I know him so well now that I readily recognize subtle body cues, the whisper of encouragement, and even the energy he brings to the set.

Eager now to perform, I need only one more thing. I need to hear the Director give his word of approval in order to proceed. His signature response of "yes, everything is in place and ready to begin." All the actors, including myself, breathe a collective sigh. Whatever happens tonight may well resonate with me for a lifetime.

The deeper meaning

If my dream last night had been a movie and me its leading actress, I would surely have won an Academy award. With a long list of credits to my honor, a great supporting cast and many well-written plays under my belt, I would receive accolades for having accomplished what might singularly appear to others as impossible.

I immediately recognize the importance of the accomplished Director, Playwright and Conductor who oversee the production. My life is in their hands and nothing I do on my own will ever conceive of such greatness.

Do I admit now to you the reader who the overseers of the play are? Why not! The Director is Father God, the Playwright is Jesus Christ, and the Conductor is the Holy Spirit.

What an amazing concept – what an amazing God and creator we have! Psalm 40:5 says it so well, *"Many, oh Lord my God are the wonders You have done. The things You planned for us no one can recount to You; were I to speak of them, they would be too many to declare." (NIV)*

Through my dreams God has revealed His creative nature. He has painted colorful landscapes; tested my resolve for adventure; and expressed His concerns for my day to day life in a way no other being could. There can be only one conclusion for me. Dreams are written in the night by His hand. I hear my God whispering to me and I become a captive audience of one.

Understand this, when dreams appear in the night they carry the potential for a dramatic release of twists and turns, drama, comedic scenes, hidden innuendos and any combination of events. All are worthy of the best cinema event. You may find yourself performing amazing feats of bravery and athletic ability and still live to fight another day.

You may even witness regions your waking imagination never considered exploring rivaling anything you may have read in the book "Alice in Wonderland". Your emotions can ride on a crest of bravery and fearlessness or remorse and melancholy; always participating, but not necessarily getting to choose.

You can partake and discover new heights of freedom and soar with eagles or tumble down canyons of fear wandering through endless halls of futility and defeat. Interspersed throughout your dream world of travel will be the unrecognizable, new and old acquaintances, sometimes even strange caricatures.

Your journey of discovery awaits you in a dream. Welcome to your dream world. Will this be just the beginning of your own personal dream story?

The final act reveals a hidden truth. In my place of slumber where dreams may come, I may not always be the leading actress. Yet, I do not despair because this is still my personal place where insight and messages from the subconscious realm seek expression and release. Inspiration flourishes and emotions are revealed, even healed.

Once we recognize the author of our dreams and surrender to His call, we need only to seek His wisdom. He is simply waiting for us to ask. Are you willing?

Bibliography

Dedication page:

[1]"Ducit amore patriae," Phillips family coat of arms (A lion with a gold crown on a silver shield). Motto translated" Love of Country leads me".

Chapter One: The hidden mystery behind dreams: What is a maze?"

[2]"To sleep perchance to dream", Google search on famous Shakespeare quotes, http./Literary Devices. Net.

[3]Definition of a "maze", Webster's the American Heritage Dictionary, page 809.

[4]Definition of "nom de guerre", Webster's the American Heritage Dictionary, page 891.

Chapter Two: "I just need the facts ma'am"

[5]Dragnet television series, "just the facts ma'am", Google search, http./Snopes fact checks.

Chapter Three: Developing a firm foundation

[6]Kung Fu television series, "patience grasshopper", Google search, http./YouTube.

Chapter Four: Filling in the blanks

[7]Definition of "context", Google word search dictionary.

Chapter Five: More about metaphors and symbols

[8]Definition of "metaphor", Google word search dictionary.
[9]Definition of "symbols", Google word search Wikipedia.
[10]Definition of "parable", Google word search Wikipedia.

Chapter Six: All the colors of the rainbow

[11]Elio Carlotti "Beauty is the summation..." quote, Google search, http./Urban Dictionary.com.

Chapter Seven: Becoming more aware

[12]Definition of "epiphanea", Google word search Wikipedia.

Chapter Ten: Moments in history and sparks of creativity

[13]Aristotle, "all men by nature desire to know", Google search, http./the internet classic archive.

Printed in the United States
By Bookmasters